KESARI COLOUR

MR VIVEK KUMAR PANDEY SHAMBHUNATH

ISBN 979-888546529-8

During writing this book no character & no religious are harmed written by Mr Vivek Kumar Pandey. Winner Youngest Writer Award 1st Rank In India 2020.He Is Only One Writer Can Publish 700+ Own Book That Was Greatest Successfull In His Life.In This Book Deeply Given About (Kesari) The Battle of Saragarhi was a last-stand battle fought before the Tirah Campaign between the British Raj and Afghan tribesmen. On 12 September 1897, an estimated 12,000 – 24,000 Orakzai and Afridi tribesmen were seen near Gogra, at Samana Suk, and around Saragarhi, cutting off Fort Gulistan from Fort Lockhart.This book fully colour edition books.

Contents

Foreword *vii*

1. Battle Of Saragarhi (kesari) 1

2. Kesari (2019 Film) 9

3. 10,000 Men's 15

4. Special Thanks Akshay Kumar (bio) 21

5. Battle Of Thermopylae 24

Foreword

Author biography in English :MY NAME IS VIVEK KUMAR PANDEY . I WAS BORN IN 30 SEP 2002,I AM FROM SURAT GUJARAT INDIA.MY DREAM WAS TO BE GOOD WRITERS ,MY FAMILY SUPPORTED ME TO SUCCESSFUL AND I CAN DO IT MY SELF.How do I write? That is a question, I believe, that can be honestly answered by me."CELEBRATING YOUNGEST WRITER AWARD WINNER IN GUJARAT 1ST RANK" MR PANDEY JI . I may think I did a good job writing something when in reality it could be horrible. The reader is the one who decides the quality of my writing. I do find writing to be natural to me and therefore find it to be a real challenge. My trick as a challenged writer is to do the best I can and know that I am happy with the final outcome. It may take a while to do my best and there may be quite a few problems I run into along the way.

I am not a greedy person those who are thinking about me and my self I never tried it anyone people suffering from sadness ,I trying to get promoted people suffering from happiness and joy in your Life Time. Now in current situation in India and also world people are unemployed and have no many but our indian governor help to people to get free food from ration card , i also take part in leadership team ,i am Motivational speaker , Film script writer. There was my two dream firstly writer and secondly actor & also my own film is upcoming soon i done almost completely completed script for my film .I AM GOING TO SAY WORD OF HEART TOUCH OUT PLEASE READ IT" , firstly i thanks my father he supports me in this field they always getting inspired me by own his words and behavior ,they always said that he was a biggest person in the world in future and also they purchase fruit and chocolate for me in anytime & anyway , firstly my father buy him then call me Vivek you want a chocolate i will say yes papa but how many tell me ,papa: you tell me how much i buy him i told 1 or 2 chocolate but my father purchase whole the boxes of chocolate and they get suprised me. MY FATHER WAS BORN IN " 20 SEPTEMBER" 1971 IN INDIA.

1) MY FATHER FAVORITE CLOTHES IS KURTA PAIJMA AND ALSO STYLES SHOE

2) FAVORITE SINGER IS KISHORE DA

3) FAVORITE STATE GUJARAT AND KOLKATA , HIS VILLAGE IN BIHAR

4) FAVORITE COLOR BLACK AND WHITE

THEY ALSO LOVE cricket like IPL and one day t-20 .they also like watching a News daily and heard the song daily ,they also interested in tik tok video but in current time tik tok is banned in india but also few videos are in you tube. In lockdown time my family and me very enjoy day daily. my father play daily ludo with his sister and son, daughter.they always loved tea and coffee anytime call me "। विवेक थोड़ा चाय बनाओना विवेक तुम्हारे हाथ का चाय अच्छा लगता है". I make it tea for my father but some reason after the April to june they are suffering from fever and cough , weakness on 6 June 2020 my father death. they not told me say bye bye his life. After death of 6 June on 10 june my mom and dad anniversary.but my father is Best in the world they can do anything for me please take care of father and respect it of your parents.

CHAPTER ONE

Battle of Saragarhi (Kesari)

- Battle of Saragarhi (Kesari)

1. During writing this book no character & no religious are harmed written by Mr Vivek Kumar Pandey.
2. In This Book Deeply Given About (Kesari) The Battle of Saragarhi was a last-stand battle fought before the Tirah Campaign between the British Raj and Afghan tribesmen. On 12 September 1897, an estimated 12,000 – 24,000 Orakzai and Afridi tribesmen were seen near Gogra, at Samana Suk, and around Saragarhi, cutting off Fort Gulistan from Fort Lockhart.

The Battle of Saragarhi was a last-stand battle fought before the Tirah Campaign between the British Raj and Afghan tribesmen.On 12 September 1897, an estimated 12,000 – 24,000 Orakzai and Afridi tribesmen were seen near Gogra, at Samana Suk, and around Saragarhi, cutting off Fort Gulistan from Fort Lockhart. The Afghans attacked the outpost of Saragarhi where thousands of them swarmed and surrounded the fort, preparing to assault it. Led by Havildar Ishar Singh, the 21 soldiers in the fort—all of whom were Sikhs—refused to surrender and were wiped out in a last stand. The post was recaptured two days later by another British Indian contingent.

All the 21 soldiers involved in the battle were posthumously awarded the Indian Order of Merit, which was the highest gallantry award that an Indian soldier could receive at the time. The Indian Army's 4th battalion of the Sikh Regiment commemorates the battle every year on 12 September, as Saragarhi Day.

- Saragarhi was a small village in the border district of Kohat, situated on the Samana Range, in present-day Pakistan. On 20 April 1894, the

36th Sikhs of the British Indian Army was created under the command of Colonel J. Cook,entirely composed of Jat Sikhs. In August 1897, five companies of the 36th Sikhs under Lieutenant Colonel John Haughton were sent to the northwest frontier of British India (modern-day Khyber Pakhtunkhwa) and were stationed at Samana Hills, Kurag, Sangar, Sahtop Dhar, and Saragarhi.

The British had partially succeeded in getting control of this volatile area, but tribal Pashtuns continued to attack British personnel from time to time. Thus, a series of forts, originally built by Ranjit Singh, the ruler of the Sikh Empire, were consolidated. Two of the forts were Fort Lockhart (on the Samana Range of the Hindu Kush mountains), and Fort Gulistan (Sulaiman Range), situated a few miles apart. Fort Lockhart is located . Due to the forts not being visible to each other, Saragarhi was created midway, as a heliographic communication post. The Saragarhi post, situated on a rocky ridge, consisted of a small block house with loop-holed ramparts and a signalling tower.

A general uprising by the Afghans began there in 1897 and, between 27 August and 11 September, many vigorous efforts by Pashtuns to capture the forts were thwarted by the 36th Sikhs. In 1897, insurgent and inimical activities had increased, and on 3 and 9 September Afridi tribesmen, allied with the Afghans, attacked Fort Gulistan. Both the attacks were repulsed, and a relief column from Fort Lockhart, on its return trip, reinforced the signalling detachment positioned at Saragarhi, increasing its strength to three non-commissioned officers (NCOs) and eighteen other ranks (ORs).

- The battle Sikh soldiers, c. 1890

Details of the Battle of Saragarhi are considered fairly accurate because Sepoy Gurmukh Singh signalled events to Fort Lockhart by heliograph as they occurred.Around 09:00, approximately 6,000–10,000 Afghans reach the signalling post at Saragarhi.Sepoy Gurmukh Singh signals to Colonel Haughton, situated in Fort Lockhart, that they are under attack.Haughton states he cannot send immediate help to Saragarhi.The soldiers in Saragarhi decide to fight to the last to prevent the enemy from reaching the forts.

- Sepoy Bhagwan Singh is the first soldier to be killed and Naik Lal Singh is seriously wounded.Naik Lal Singh and Sepoy Jiwa Singh reportedly carry the body of Bhagwan Singh back to the inner layer of the post.The Afghans break a portion of the wall of the picket.Haughton signals that he has estimated that there are between 10,000 and 14,000 Pashtuns attacking Saragarhi.

The leaders of the Pashtun forces reportedly make promises to the soldiers to entice them to surrender.Reportedly two determined attempts are made to rush open the gate, but are unsuccessful.Later, the wall is breached.Thereafter, some of the fiercest hand-to-hand fighting occurs.Havildar Ishar Singh orders his men to fall back into the inner layer, whilst he remains to cover their retreat. However, this is breached and all but one of the defending soldiers are killed, along with many of the Pashtuns.

Sepoy Gurmukh Singh, who communicated the battle to Haughton, is the last surviving defender. His last message is for permission to pick up his rifle. Upon receiving permission he packs up the heliograph and holds the door of his signalling shed. He is stated to have killed 40 Afghans, the Pashtuns having to set fire to the post to kill him. As he is dying, he is said to have yelled repeatedly the Sikh battle cry "Bole So Nihal, Sat Sri Akal!" ("One will be blessed eternally, who says that God is the ultimate truth!").

- Weapons

The weapons given and used by the Indian troops were of an older generation compared to the small arms issued to British troops. This was intentionally done after the Indian Mutiny of 1857 to prevent any further mutinies and uprisings from getting out of hand. The Afghans used the original and copy of Martini-Henry rifles. The Martini–Henry was copied on a large scale by North-West Frontier Province gunsmiths. The chief manufacturers were the Adam Khel Afridi, who lived around the Khyber Pass. The Khyber Pass gunsmiths first acquired examples of the various British service arms during nineteenth-century British military expeditions in the North-West Frontier, which they used to make copies.

- Soldiers

The names of the 21 Sikh soldiers were

1. Havildar Ishar Singh (regimental number 165)
2. Naik Lal Singh (332)
3. Lance Naik Chanda Singh (546)
4. Sepoy Sundar Singh (1321)
5. Sepoy Ramm Singh (287)
6. Sepoy Uttar Singh (492)
7. Sepoy Sahib Singh (182)
8. Sepoy Hira Singh (359)
9. Sepoy Daya Singh (687)
10. Sepoy Jivan Singh (760)
11. Sepoy Bhola Singh (791)
12. Sepoy Narayan Singh (834)
13. Sepoy Gurmukh Singh (814)
14. Sepoy Jivan Singh (871)
15. Sepoy Gurmukh Singh (1733)
16. Sepoy Ram Singh (163)
17. Sepoy Bhagwan Singh (1257)
18. Sepoy Bhagwan Singh (1265)
19. Sepoy Buta Singh (1556)
20. Sepoy Jivan Singh (1651)
21. Sepoy Nand Singh (1221)

- Aftermath

Having destroyed Saragarhi, the Afghans turned their attention to Fort Gulistan, but they had been delayed too long, and reinforcements arrived there in the night of 13–14 September, before the fort could be captured. The Pashtuns later admitted that they had lost about 180 killed and many more wounded during the engagement against the 21 Sikh soldiers. Some 600 bodies are said to have been seen around the ruined post when the relief party arrived (however, the fort had been retaken, on 14 September, by the use of intensive artillery fire, which may have caused some casualties). The total casualties in the entire campaign, including the Battle of Saragarhi, numbered at around 4,800.

- The inscription of a commemorative tablet reads

The Government of India have caused this tablet to be erected to the memory of the twenty one non-commissioned officers and men of the 36 Sikh Regiment of the Bengal Infantry whose names are engraved below as a perpetual record of the heroism shown by these gallant soldiers who died at their posts in the defense of the fort of Saragarhi, on the 12 September 1897, fighting against overwhelming numbers, thus proving their loyalty and devotion to their sovereign The Queen Empress of India and gloriously maintaining the reputation of the Sikhs for unflinching courage on the field of battle.

- Order of Merit

The 21 Sikh non-commissioned officers and soldiers who died in the Battle of Saragarhi were from the Majha region of Punjab and were posthumously awarded the Indian Order of Merit, at that time the highest gallantry award which an Indian soldier could receive. The corresponding gallantry award was the Victoria Cross. The award is equivalent to today's Param Vir Chakra awarded by the President of India.

- Saragarhi Memorial Gurdwara, built in 1904

The battle has become iconic of eastern military civilisation, the British Empire's military history and Sikh history. The modern Sikh Regiment of the Indian Army continues to commemorate the Battle of Saragarhi on 12 September each year as the Regimental Battle Honours Day.

To commemorate the men, the British built two Saragarhi Gurdwaras: one in Amritsar, very close to the main entrance of the Golden Temple, and another in Firozpur Cantonment, in the district that most of the men hailed from.The epic poem "Khalsa Bahadur" is in memory of the Sikhs who died at Saragarhi.

- In Indian schools

The Indian Armed Forces, in particular the Indian Army, has been pushing for the battle to be taught in India's schools. They would like the heroism demonstrated by the Indian soldiers to be taught as an inspiration to children. In 1999, various articles were printed regarding the matter in Punjab's longest-established newspaper, The Tribune, such as: "the military action at Saragarhi is taught to students the world over and particularly to students in France." Although there seems to be no evidence for this claim (it is not, for example, on France's national school curriculum), the news was enough to provoke political debate, and the battle has been taught in schools in Punjab since 2000:

The decision to include the battle story in the school curriculum was taken last year during a public rally presided over by the Punjab Chief Minister, Mr Parkash Singh Badal. Following this, the State Government had issued a notification that the battle story should be included in the school curriculum from this session. There had been a constant demand from the Sikh Regiment and various ex-servicemen's associations that the battle be included in the school curriculum. A similar request had also been put forward to Mr Badal during the battle's state-level centenary celebrations at Ferozepore in 1997. A subsequent letter sent to the Punjab Government by the Saragarhi Memorial and Ethos Promotion Forum had also urged the State Government that the battle has many inspiring lessons for children. On hearing the acts of valour, the British Parliament had then risen in unison to pay homage to the fallen soldiers.

- Saragarhi Day

Saragarhi Day is a Sikh military commemoration day celebrated on 12 September every year to commemorate the Battle of Saragarhi. Sikh military personnel and civilians commemorate the battle around the world every year on 12 September. All units of the Sikh Regiment celebrate Saragarhi Day every year as the Regimental Battle Honours Day.

- Saragarhi Day in the UK

The first recorded public discourse on Saragarhi was delivered by Viscount Slim in 2001 when he delivered the annual Portraits of Courage lecture at the Imperial War Museum. This was hosted by the Maharaja Duleep Singh Centenary Trust. In May 2002, Prince Charles inaugurated the Jawans to Generals exhibition which featured a section on Saragarhi. The exhibition successfully toured the UK and was seen by over 100,000 visitors.

Saragarhi was introduced back into the UK by writer and filmmaker Jay Singh Sohal and the British Army with the launch of the book Saragarhi:

The Forgotten Battle in 2013 at Old College, Royal Military Academy Sandhurst.It has since been commemorated each year on its battle honour day by the British Armed Forces. In 2014, the commemoration also took place at Sandhurst at the Indian Army Memorial Room. In 2015, it took place at the Honourable Artillery Company Museum in London, where was also due to take place in 2016.

Various senior ministers and armed forces generals have paid tribute to Sikh service by mentioning the story of Saragarhi. In April 2016 the Defence Secretary Michael Fallon MP made mention as a special Vaisakhi event at the Ministry of Defence. In June 2016 the Chief of the General Staff Sir Nick Carter did the same at a special British Sikh Association dinner.

In November 2020, Wolverhampton City Council approved plans for the erection of a 10 ft tall bronze statue commemorating the battle outside of the Guru Nanak Gurdwara in Wednesfield. The statue of Havildar Ishar Singh, paid for by donations from the local Sikh community totalling £100,000, was unveiled on 12 September 2021.

- In popular culture

In September 2017, Saragarhi: The True Story, a documentary by UK-based journalist-filmmaker Jay Singh-Sohal, was screened at the National Memorial Arboretum in Staffordshire to mark the 120th anniversary of the epic frontier battle.

A TV series, 21 Sarfarosh - Saragarhi 1897 aired on Discovery Jeet from 12 February 2018 to 11 May 2018, starring Mohit Raina, Mukul Dev, and Balraj Singh Khehra.

Kesari (2019) is a film directed by Anurag Singh, starring Akshay Kumar, that grossed over 100 crore worldwide in its opening weekend during the Holi festival. Two other Bollywood films based on the battle had been announced prior to Kesari:

Sons of Sardaar: The Battle of Saragarhi. In July 2016, Ajay Devgn shared a poster of the film, a sequel to Son of Sardaar. In August 2017, Devgn stated: "We are working on the script but it won't happen for another two years because of the scale of the project."

Battle of Saragarhi. In August 2016, Randeep Hooda shared the first look on his Twitter page. This film is to be directed by Rajkumar Santoshi, starring Hooda, Vikramjeet Virk, and Danny Denzongpa. The film was shelved after the release of Kesari.

Regarding speculation about many films being made about the battle, Hooda stated: "It is good because there were 21 Sikh heroes in that battle and each one of them deserved to have a movie made on them. So actually there should be 21 films made on them."

CHAPTER TWO

Kesari (2019 film)

- Kesari (2019 film)

Kesari (transl. Saffron) is a 2019 Indian Hindi-language war film written and directed by Anurag Singh. It was jointly produced by Aruna Bhatia, Karan Johar, Hiroo Yash Johar, Apoorva Mehta, and Sunir Khetarpal under the banners of Dharma Productions, Cape of Good Films, Azure Entertainment, and Zee Studios. The film stars Akshay Kumar with Parineeti Chopra in a special appearance, Vikram Singh Chauhan, Sarwar, Vansh Bhardwaj, Jaspreet Singh, Vivek Saini, Vikram Kochhar, and Rakesh Sharma in supporting roles. It follows the events leading to the Battle of Saragarhi, a battle between 21 soldiers of the 36th Sikhs of the British Indian Army and 10,000 Afridi and Orakzai Pashtun tribesmen in 1897.

- Initially planned as a production collaboration between Salman Khan and Johar with Kumar starring in the lead role, Kesari was announced in October 2017, with Kumar and Johar reprising their responsibilities; Khan later quit the project. Parineeti Chopra was cast as the wife of Kumar's character. Principal photography for the film began in January 2018 and concluded in December. The soundtrack was composed by Tanishk Bagchi, Arko Pravo Mukherjee, Chirantan Bhatt, Jasbir Jassi, Gurmoh and Jasleen Royal with lyrics written by Kumaar, Manoj Muntashir, Kunwar Juneja and Bagchi. Produced on a budget of 80 crore (equivalent to 84 crore or US$11 million in 2020), the film was distributed internationally by Zee Studios.

The film was released in India during the Holi festival, on 21 March 2019. It received positive reviews from critics, who appreciated performances of ensemble cast, visuals, production values, art direction, action sequences, and tribute, it had a good start at the box office, while the opening day morning collection was affected by Holi-related celebrations. The film grossed over 100 crore worldwide in its opening weekend. It grossed over 207.09 crores worldwide, becoming one of the highest-grossing Bollywood films of 2019.

- Plot

Havildar Ishar Singh is a part of the Sikh Regiment of the British Indian Army posted at Gulistan fort along with the British-held territories, and Afghan border. A British officer is jealous of him because of his superior fighting skills and thinks little of the native Indians, deeming them to be cowards. While just returning from a border patrol, the troop sees a group of Afghan tribesmen led by Saidullah trying to kill a married Afghan woman who does not acknowledge her forced marriage. Ishar Singh intervenes, fights off the tribesmen, and rescues the woman by killing her husband, thereby disobeying his immediate superior.

Once the troop reaches the base fort, the British officer reports Ishar Singh's disobedience to his commanding officer who sits at the nearby Lockhart fort. The Afghans then attack the British-controlled Gulistan fort but are stopped by Ishar Singh who fights valiantly, killing many Afghans. He is punished and transferred to Saragarhi Fort that sits between Gulistan and Lockhart fort and enables communication between them. When Ishar Singh's transfer orders are issued, he travels to Saragarhi fort and upon arriving there finds the troop in a mess. He enforces discipline in the troop by punishing all to live without food for an entire week. The troop initially is furious but later respects Ishar Singh on learning that he too was living without food. Meanwhile, Saidullah forms an alliance between the Afghan tribes and motivates them to mount an attack on British territories as a unified force. Ishar Singh and Lal Singh go to a nearby village in search of their informant who hadn't reported to them for over three days.

The British Commanding Officer Col. John Haughton from Lockhart fort sees the Afghan Forces marching towards Sargarhi and alerts Ishar. Ishar and his battalion find some ten thousand tribesmen encircling the fort. Saidullah, with the entire Afghan army at his back, kills the woman Ishar Singh had rescued earlier in front of the Saragarhi Fort. Despite the commanding officer's orders to abandon the fort and flee, Ishar Singh and his men decide to fight till their death. Ishar Singh deploys his force in position. Khuda Daad volunteers to fight but Ishar Singh asks him to instead provide water to the injured soldiers (Including the Afghans).

The Afghans initiate the battle, and Bhagwan Singh is the first to be killed. Gurmukh Singh being an inexperienced soldier, is unable to fight, due to which Ishar Singh asks him to keep the CO updated regarding the battle, and decides to prolong the battle so as to prevent the Afghans from advancing to the Gulistan and Lockhart forts. As the battle prolongs, Lal Singh alone fights the Afghans outside the fort and dies while asking one of the sepoys to close the gate to the fort. Meanwhile, the Afghans manage to destroy the back wall of the fort using explosives.

Ishar Singh remembers his wife Jeevani one last time after removing the stripes from his uniform and starts fighting the Afghans with a red-hot sword before he gets fatally stabbed. Saidullah kills Khuda Daad before himself being stabbed to death by Ishar while trying to remove his turban. Ishar's bravery impresses an Afghan chieftain who orders his men not to touch any Sikh's turban. One of the Afghan chieftains named Gul Badshah, orders the signaling post to be lit up so Gurmukh Singh's painful screams can be heard as a consolation. As the Afghans set the post on fire, Gurmukh Singh emerges with his body on fire. He chants "Bole So Nihal, Sat Sri Akaal" thrice, grabs Gul Badshah and triggers the grenades attached to his body, resulting in a huge explosion. The shout echoes and reaches both the nearby forts. The Sikh soldiers present there also start chanting in the name of their Guru.

The surviving Afghans loot the fort and eventually set it on fire. The British Parliament honors the martyrs with a two-minute silence and posthumously awards them the British Order of Merit, at that time the highest gallantry award an Indian soldier could receive, with the Victoria Cross being the corresponding one.

- Cast

1. Akshay Kumar as Havildar Ishar Singh
2. Hani Yadav as Rohan Chopra as Hawaldar inspector
3. Parineeti Chopra as Jeevani Kaur
4. Mir Sarwar as Khan Masud
5. Ashwath Bhatt as Gul Badshah Khan
6. Rakesh Chaturvedi as Mullah Saidullah

7. Hariom kalra as afgani tribal sardar
8. Vivek Saini as Sep. Jiwan Singh
9. Pritpal Pali Sep. Gurmukh singh
10. Vikram Kochhar as Sep. Gulab Singh
11. Suvinder Vicky as Nk. Lal Singh
12. Vansh Bharadwaj as L/Nk. Chanda Singh
13. Ravinder Pawar as Sep. Attar Singh
14. Surmeet Singh Basra as Sep. Gurmukh Singh
15. Ajit Singh Mahela as Sep. Nand Singh
16. Sandeep Nahar as Sep. Buta Singh
17. Harvinder Singh as Sep. Daya Singh
18. Rakesh Sharma as Sep. Bhola Singh
19. Adhrit Sharma as Sep. Uttam Singh
20. Harbhagwan Singh as Sep. Bhaghwan Singh
21. Rajdeep Singh Dhaliwal as Sep. Ram Singh
22. Gurpreet Toti as Sep. Saheb Singh
23. Harry Brar as Sep. Sunder Singh
24. Pali Sandhu as Sep. Narayan Singh
25. Vikram Singh Chauhan as Sep. Hira Singh
26. Gugneet Singh as Sep. Jiwan Singh
27. Jaspreet Singh as Taklu
28. Toranj Kayvon as Gulwarien
29. Edward Sonnenblick as Lt. Lawrence
30. R. Bhakti Klein as Major Des-Voeux
31. Brahma Mishra as Daad
32. Muzamil Bhawani as Marksman/Sniper

- Production & Development

In 2017, Salman Khan and Karan Johar announced that they would be producing a film together based on the Battle of Saragarhi starring Akshay Kumar in the lead role. Media reports later speculated Khan left the project in favor of a similarly themed film starring Ajay Devgn, and in October that year, Johar and Kumar announced a statement about their collaboration on the film; that Khan had quit the film, and that it would be titled Kesari. Parineeti Chopra was confirmed for a minor role as the wife of Kumar's character, whom he had left behind at the village after joining the army.

- Marketing and release

Kumar released Kesari's first look poster on 12 September 2018, through Twitter. Another poster was released on India's Republic Day, 26 January 2019.The film's theatrical poster was released on 11 February 2019.

The following day, Dharma Productions released three videos titled "Glimpses of Kesari" on their YouTube channel, detailing the film's production. A second theatrical release poster for Kesari was released on 20 February 2019.

The first song of the film "Sanu Kehndi" was released on 27 February 2019, the second one "Teri Mitti" was released on 15 March 2019 and the full album was released on 18 March 2019.Kesari was released worldwide during the Indian Holi festival, on 21 March 2019. It had a release on 4200 screens worldwide, 3600 screens of which were in India and the rest overseas.

- Critical response

Rachit Gupta of The Times of India gave Kesari four stars out of five, praising its "technical brilliance, intricate writing and thundering performances". Taran Adarsh gave it four stars and felt it "chronicles a significant chapter from history brilliantly... Nationalism, patriotism, heroism, scale and soul – Kesari has it all". Writing for Times Now, Gaurang Chauhan rated the film three and a half stars out of five and opined, "Kesari is not the best patriotic film or action film to come out of Bollywood, but it surely is worth the time and money". Bollywood Hungama rated it four stars out of five, remarking.

"On the whole, Kesari is a brave and inspirational tale of courage, with patriotism and the dramatic battle sequences being the USP of the film".Nandini Ramnath of Scroll.in writes, "Sluggishly paced until the interval and springing to life only in fits and starts in the second half, Kesari is a poor attempt to revisit a chapter in Indian military history that earned the admiration even of British colonizers." Though mainly positively received in India, the film was negatively received in the Muslim world, which saw the film's portrayal of the main antagonist as a Muslim maulana, as well as displaying rancor against a Sikh turban by Muslim Afghans as little more than Hindu Nationalist.=

- Kesari Box office

Kesari opened with collection of 210.6 million on its first day. The collection of extended weekend of the film is 780.7 million, which was the highest opening weekend collection of 2019 for Bollywood films released till May. Its domestic gross was 182.30 crore and overseas gross 24.79 crore. It has grossed 207.09 crore worldwide. The film grossed over 100 crore worldwide in its opening weekend. It became the fastest 100 crore earning film in domestic net in 2019 for Bollywood films released till May. It eventually grossed over 200 crore (equivalent to 211 crore or US$28 million in 2020) worldwide in its fourth week.

CHAPTER THREE

10,000 Men's

- Captain Jay Singh-Sohal explores the events of 12 September 1897 at the battle of Saragarhi – which saw a British outpost surrounded by 10,000 Afghan tribesmen – and shares the remarkable story of a valiant last stand that would reverberate around the British empire...

In the late 19th century, tensions were heightened between Britain and Russia as the nations battled over territories in central Asia. British forces held vulnerable posts on the colonial border between British India and Afghanistan, threatened by both Russian forces and Afghan tribes. Here, Captain Jay Singh-Sohal explores the events of 12 September 1897 at the battle of Saragarhi...

The frontier between colonial India and Afghanistan in the 19th century was a place of danger and unrest. In 1897, at a small outpost called Saragarhi, 40 miles away from the British garrison town of Kohat (in what is now Pakistan), 21 Sikh soldiers stood their ground against an onslaught of 10,000 enemy tribesmen. Their gallantry in fighting to the bitter end cemented their reputation as brave and devoted to their duty, and the soldiers were recognised by the British with memorials, a battle honour and a regimental holiday. So why was Saragarhi viewed with such significance, and how is it still relevant today?

The timing of the battle is crucial: it occurred during the period of the 19th century known as the 'Great Game', the name given to the heightened tensions between Britain and Russia as they battled over Afghanistan and other territories in central Asia.

- The story of the Bayeux Tapestry

From 1881 to 1885, as the Russians penetrated eastwards in Turkestan, efforts were made to avoid all-out war. A compromise was reached between the two in 1885: a boundary commission was set up in British India with agreement from the emir of Afghanistan, Abdur Rahman Khan, in order to finally define spheres of British and Afghan influence. This later became the Durrand Line, which is still in dispute today. Following the agreement, Britain developed a 'forward policy' of occupying frontier lands and keeping a presence in places inhabited by Pathans, the tribes of people residing in the region.

General Sir Frederick Roberts' troops behind fortifications at Kabul during the Second Afghan War, 1878-1880.

- A new British post at Saragarhi

In 1891, Brigadier General Sir William Lockhart led two expeditions of the Miranzai Field Force on to the Samana [a mountain range] in order to bring the tribes there under British rule, aiming eventually to build forts on the high ground of the Mastan plateau. By May, a memorandum was issued by the commander-in-chief of India, General Sir Frederick Roberts (later First Baron Roberts of Kandahar) on the posts and roads to be created for the military occupation of the range.

Two new main forts of Lockhart and Gulistan were placed on vital ground. Other smaller 'picquet' posts were built nearby, including on the high part of the main range, west of the village of Saragarhi. Roberts's memorandum stated this post, which was situated a mile and half west of Lockhart and a mile and three-quarters east of Gulistan, should be visible from both forts. Saragarhi was the most important of the picquets because through it, heliographic signal communications – signals using flashes of sunlight – could be maintained between the two main forts.

While the telegraph had been invented much earlier in 1835 by Samuel Morse, the heliograph became a necessary means of sending Morse code on the frontier. While field telegraphs had been put up between Lockhart and Gulistan, the wire laid beneath the ground to carry these messages was continually cut by the locals. When they were repaired, the enemy persevered, so it became necessary to develop another means of sending messages. The heliograph at Saragarhi would send Morse code through the use of flashing lights.

- A regiment to combat 'tribal agitation'

The regiment sent to the Samana was the 36th (Sikh) Regiment of Bengal Infantry. It was raised in March 1887 specifically for service along the unruly north west frontier with the intent of checking tribal agitation. The unit (and its sister regiment, the 35th Sikhs) were raised by Colonel Jim Cooke and the infamous Captain Henry Holmes, the latter being the biggest and strongest man of his time in the Indian army. It is said that he challenged men in Ludhiana, Punjab, to a wrestling match, with the proviso that if they lost, they would enlist. This novel way of recruitment saw young men flock to try and beat the Brit. While recruitment was taking place across Punjab, 225 men were also brought over to the regiment from other units of the Punjab Frontier Force and Bengal Army, bringing the 36th to full strength of 912 men in eight companies by January 1888.

After a period of training and domestic movements, the regiment was eventually led in January 1897 by its commander, Lt Col John Haughton (the son of an Afghan war hero of the same name), to occupy the Samana posts.

- While the 36th Sikhs took to their daily duties, the action of drawing boundaries on the frontier led to the Afridi people of nearby Tirah rising up in defiance of the peace they had held for 16 years with the British. By August 1897 the Mullah of Hadda, an influential preacher, had declared a jihad "to go out for a holy war and defend the religion of the Holy Prophet". The Afridis convinced their neighbouring Orakzai clan to join the cause and marched on the Samana.

A reconnaissance patrol sent out to the Samana Suk [the highest peak of the mountain range] on 9 September found that a strong force of tribesmen was assembled near Khangarbur; 29 standards were counted, giving an indication of enemy numbers. The next day more enemies arrived, pushing estimates to 25,000.

Haughton's 36th Sikhs were spread along the picquets and forts: 168 soldiers were at Lockhart under his command, while 175 rifles were at Gulistan under Major Charles Des Voeux. The picquet at Dhar contained 37, and Sartop and Saragarhi both contained 21 Sikhs; the latter also held a camp follower named Dadh, who cleaned and cooked for the regiment.

A British soldier signalling with a heliograph, dated 19th century.

- A surrounded post

The enemy surrounded Saragarhi on 12 September, knowing full well that this would cut communications and troop movements between the forts of Lockhart and Gulistan, and that with the British forces spread out it would no longer be possible for Haughton to send aid. The 22 men inside were led by an experienced sergeant in Havildar Ishar Singh, who rallied his men to defend their positions.

The Pathans attacked at around 9AM, but were repulsed with around 60 losses as the Sikhs fired upon the mass of men. The enemy dived behind rocks and dips in the ground for cover, but two tribesmen had also managed to get to the post and remained close under the walls of the north-west bastion where there was a dead angle

- Viceroy's House: the history behind the film

Unseen by the Sikhs inside, they began digging beneath the walls. The enemy next set fire to bushes and shrubbery to create a smokescreen with which to edge forward. They concentrated their gunfire on the wooden front door, a defect of planning which presented a weakness.

A signaller, Gurmukh Singh, messaged an account of events, though he did not pick up any incoming messages from Major Des Vouex at Gulistan, who could see the diggers clearly and was trying in vain to alert Saragarhi to the danger. The smokescreen may account for why he did not pick up the flashes, although light is known to penetrate through such haze. More likely is that he was unable to do so, as he was just one man, doing the job of three. Heliography required at least three men: one to flash messages using the mirror; another to read out incoming messages; and a third to write it all down. It is not impossible that Gurmukh Singh could have done all, but the pressure of the situation made it unlikely.

Haughton too tried several times to sally forward with a party of rifles to divert the enemy away from Saragarhi, but the sheer number of tribesmen meant he could not get far without being outflanked. The Sikhs continued to hold back the enemy but by noon, one sepoy [an infantryman in the British Indian army] had been killed and another wounded, with three rifles broken by enemy gunfire.

- A familiar tragedy: Britain's first war in Afghanistan

The battle culminated at around 3PM when a section of wall under attack from the diggers began to cave in; the enemy gave a final cry to advance and rushed through the new gap. As the enemy crowded over their own dead and injured to get into Saragarhi, the few Sikhs remaining inside put up a stubborn defence but were forced to retreat into the inner defences. Ishar Singh is believed to have covered the retreat and engaged in hand-to-hand combat. Another sepoy secured the guardroom door from the inside and carried on firing, but was burned to death in an ensuing fire. The signaller Gurmukh Singh is said to have asked permission to pack away his equipment before joining the fight.The 21 Sikhs had made a valiant last stand, and the enemy had paid a high price for their victory, with around 180 dead.

- 'Gallant soldiers'

The heliograph, the reason why the men fought to defend Saragarhi, would ironically be the source of their fame: details of their heroism were heliographed and then telegraphed back to London by a Times correspondent and then reported in newspapers around the world. The commander-in-chief of India recorded his "admiration of the heroism shown by those gallant soldiers".

The British saw the significance of this last stand in inspiring more Indians to serve and fight, and built two Memorial Gurdwaras: one near Sri Harimandir Sahib (Golden Temple), Amritsar, and another in Ferozepur. The 36th Sikhs were duly rewarded a battle honour for the Samana and 12 September was set as a regimental holiday.

- This commemoration continues to be marked in India by the descendant 4 Sikh Regiment while the chief minister of Punjab, Captain Amarinder Singh, has recently invoked a Punjab-wide holiday for the battle on 12 September.

Saragarhi is now officially commemorated in the UK too, and other forgotten frontier battles are gaining more attention. This year, for the 120th anniversary, the annual commemoration event will be held at the National Memorial Arboretum, home of the UK's inaugural First World War Sikh Memorial, to remember and honour all those who fought and died on the forgotten frontier.

Captain Jay Singh-Sohal is the author of Saragarhi: The Forgotten Battle (2013) and presenter of the new documentary film Saragarhi: The True Story released on 12 September 2017. He is a journalist and serves as an Army reserve officer.

CHAPTER FOUR

Special Thanks AKSHAY KUMAR (BIO)

- Akshay Kumar

Rajiv Hari Om Bhatia (born 9 September 1967), known professionally as Akshay Kumar is an Indian-born naturalised Canadian actor, film producer, and television personality who works in Bollywood, the commercial Hindi language film industry based mainly in Mumbai. Over 29 years, Kumar has appeared in over 100 films and has won several awards, including a National Film Award for Best Actor and two Filmfare Awards. Kumar is one of the most successful prolific actors of Hindi cinema. Having starred in 113 films, 52 of which were commercially successful, he was the first Bollywood actor whose films' domestic net lifetime collections crossed 20 billion (US$270 million) by 2013, and 30 billion (US$400 million) by 2016.

Kumar began his career in 1991 with Saugandh, but his first mainstream success came a year later with the action thriller Khiladi. The film established him as an action star in the 1990s and was the first of several films starring Kumar which would later become commonly known as the Khiladi film series, in addition to a string of other action films. Although his early tryst with romance in Yeh Dillagi (1994) was positively received, it was in the next decade that Kumar expanded his range of roles. He gained recognition for the romantic films Dhadkan (2000), Andaaz (2003) and Namastey London (2007), as well as drama films such as Waqt (2005) and Patiala House (2011). His comic performances in films such as Hera Pheri (2000), Mujhse Shaadi Karogi (2004), Bhool Bhulaiyaa (2007) and Singh Is Kinng (2008) met with acclaim.

- Kumar won Filmfare Awards for his negative role in Ajnabee (2001) and his comic performance in Garam Masala (2005). While his career had fluctuated commercially, his mainstream success soared in 2007 with four consecutive box-office hits in India; it was consistent until a short period of professional setbacks between 2009 and 2011, after which he reinforced his status with several films, including Rowdy Rathore (2012) and Holiday (2014). Moreover, around this time the critical response to several of his films improved; after favourable reviews came his way for his work in Special 26 (2013), Baby and Airlift (2016), he won the National Film Award for Best Actor for his performance in the crime thriller Rustom (2016). He earned further notice for the social films Toilet: Ek Prem Katha (2017) and Pad Man (2018) and the war film Kesari (2019).

Apart from acting, Kumar has worked as a stunt actor; he has often performed many dangerous stunts in his films, which has earned him the sobriquet "Indian Jackie Chan". In 2008, he hosted the show Fear Factor: Khatron Ke Khiladi. In 2008, the University of Windsor conferred an honorary doctorate on Kumar. In 2009, he was awarded the Padma Shri the fourth-highest civil honour by the Government of India. In 2009, he founded the Hari Om Entertainment production company and Grazing Goat Pictures production company in 2012. In 2014, Kumar launched the TV reality show Dare 2 Dance. He also owns the team Khalsa Warriors in the World Kabaddi League. As of 2015 and 2019, Kumar was on the Forbes list of highest paid entertainers in the world, ranking 52nd with earnings of $48.5 million. and the only Bollywood actor on the list.n 2020, he was ranked as the highest paid Bollywood actor by Forbes.

Sometime during or after the 2011 Canadian federal election, the Conservative government granted Canadian citizenship to Kumar by invoking a little-known law which allowed circumventing the usual residency requirement for Canadian immigrants. According to a former Conservative Party minister, Tony Clement, the citizenship was awarded in return for Kumar's offer of putting his "star power to use to advance Canada-Indian relations", and Canada's "trade relations, commercial relations, in the movie sector, in the tourism sector".

- Akshay Kumar life

Kumar was born in Amritsar, Punjab, India, to Hari Om Bhatia and Aruna Bhatia in a Punjabi family. His father was an army officer.From a young age, Kumar was very interested in sports. His father too enjoyed wrestling. He lived and grew up in Delhi's Chandni Chowk and later he moved to Bombay (present-day Mumbai) when his father left Army to become an accountant with UNICEF.Soon, his sister was born and the family lived in Koliwada, a Punjabi dominated area of Central Bombay.

He received his school education from Don Bosco High School, Matunga, simultaneously learning Karate. He enrolled in Guru Nanak Khalsa College for higher education, but dropped out as he was not much interested in studies. He requested his father that he wanted to learn martial arts further, and his father somehow saved money to send him to Thailand. Kumar went to Bangkok to learn martial arts and lived in Thailand for five years learning Thai Boxing. Kumar also has a sister, Alka Bhatia. When Kumar was a teenager, his father asked him what he aspired to be. Kumar expressed his desire to become an actor.

After having obtained a black belt in Taekwondo while in India, he studied martial arts in Bangkok, Thailand, where he learned Muay Thai and worked as a chef and waiter.After Thailand, Kumar went to work in Calcutta (present-day Kolkata) in a travel agency, in Dhaka in a hotel as a chef and Delhi where he sold Kundan jewellery. Upon his return to Bombay, he commenced the teaching of martial arts.

During this time, the father of one of his students, himself a model co-ordinator, recommended Kumar into modelling which ultimately led to a modelling assignment for a furniture showroom. Kumar effectively made more money within the first two days of shooting than in his entire month's salary, and therefore chose a modelling career path. He worked as an assistant for photographer Jayesh Sheth for 18 months without payment to shoot his first portfolio. He also worked as a background dancer in various films. One morning, he missed his flight for an ad-shoot in Bangalore. Disappointed with himself, he visited a film studio along with his portfolio. That evening, Kumar was signed for a lead role by producer Pramod Chakravarthy for the movie Deedar.

CHAPTER FIVE

Battle of Thermopylae

- Battle of Thermopylae
- This war not related to kesari only for knowledge

The Battle of Thermopylae was fought between an alliance of Ancient Greek city-states, led by King Leonidas I of Sparta, and the Achaemenid Empire of Xerxes I. It was fought in 480 BC over the course of three days, during the second Persian invasion of Greece.

- The battle took place simultaneously with the naval battle at Artemisium. It occurred at the narrow coastal pass of Thermopylae ("The Hot Gates") in August or September 480 BC. The Persian invasion was a delayed response to the defeat of the first Persian invasion of Greece, which had been ended by the Athenian victory at the Battle of Marathon in 490 BC. By 480 BC, Xerxes had amassed a massive army and navy and set out to conquer all of Greece. The Athenian politician and general Themistocles had proposed that the allied Greeks block the advance of the Persian army at the pass of Thermopylae, while simultaneously blocking the Persian navy at the Straits of Artemisium.

A Greek force of approximately 7,000 men marched north to block the pass in the middle of 480 BC. The Persian army was rumoured to have numbered over one million soldiers. Herodotus, a contemporary writer, put the Persian army strength as one million and went to great pains to describe how they were counted in groups of ten thousand at a review of the troops. Simonides went as far as to put the Persian number at three million. Today, it is considered to have been much smaller. Scholars report various figures ranging between about 100,000 and 150,000 soldiers.

- The Persian army arrived at the pass in late August or early September. The vastly outnumbered Greeks held them off for seven days (including three of battle) before the rear-guard was annihilated in one of history's most famous last stands. During two full days of battle, the small force led by Leonidas blocked the only road by which the massive Persian army could pass. After the second day, a local resident named Ephialtes betrayed the Greeks by revealing a small path used by shepherds. It led the Persians behind the Greek lines. Leonidas, aware that his force was being outflanked, dismissed the bulk of the Greek army and remained to guard their retreat with 300 Spartans and 700 Thespians. It has been reported that others also remained, including up to 900 helots and 400 Thebans. With the exception of the Thebans, most of whom reportedly surrendered, the Greeks fought to the death.

Themistocles was in command of the Greek navy at Artemisium when he received news that the Persians had taken the pass at Thermopylae. Since the Greek strategy required both Thermopylae and Artemisium to be held, given their losses, it was decided to withdraw to Salamis. The Persians overran Boeotia and then captured the evacuated city of Athens. The Greek fleet—seeking a decisive victory over the Persian armada—attacked and defeated the invaders at the Battle of Salamis in late 480 BC. Wary of being trapped in Europe, Xerxes withdrew with much of his army to Asia (losing most to starvation and disease), leaving Mardonius to attempt to complete the conquest of Greece. However, the following year saw a Greek army decisively defeat the Persians at the Battle of Plataea, thereby ending the Persian invasion.

Both ancient and modern writers have used the Battle of Thermopylae as an example of the power of an army defending its native soil. The performance of the defenders is also used as an example of the advantages of training, equipment, and good use of terrain as force multipliers.

- Herodotus

The primary source for the Greco-Persian Wars is the Greek historian Herodotus. The Sicilian historian Diodorus Siculus, writing in the 1st century BC in his Bibliotheca historica, also provides an account of the Greco-Persian wars, partially derived from the earlier Greek historian Ephorus. This account is fairly consistent with Herodotus' writings. The

Greco-Persian Wars, are also described in less detail by a number of other ancient historians including Plutarch, Ctesias of Cnidus, and are referred to by other authors, as in Aeschylus in The Persians.

Archaeological evidence, such as the Serpent Column (now in the Hippodrome of Constantinople), also supports some of Herodotus' specific claims. George B. Grundy was the first modern historian to do a thorough topographical survey of the narrow pass at Thermopylae, and to the extent that modern accounts of the battle differ from Herodotus' where they usually follow Grundy's.For example, the military strategist Sir Basil Henry Liddell Hart defers to Grundy. Grundy also explored Plataea and wrote a treatise on that battle.

On the Battle of Thermopylae itself, two principal sources, Herodotus' and Simonides' accounts, survive. In fact, Herodotus' account of the battle, in Book VII of his Histories, is such an important source that Paul Cartledge wrote: "we either write a history of Thermopylae with Herodotus, or not at all". Also surviving is an epitome of the account of Ctesias, by the eighth-century Byzantine Photios, though this is "almost worse than useless",missing key events in the battle such as the betrayal of Ephialtes, and the account of Diodorus Siculus in his Universal History. Diodorus' account seems to have been based on that of Ephorus and contains one significant deviation from Herodotus' account: a supposed night attack against the Persian camp, of which modern scholars have tended to be skeptical.

- A map of almost all the parts of the Greek world that partook in the Persian Wars

The Athenian city-states of Athens and Eretria had aided the unsuccessful Ionian Revolt against the Persian Empire of Darius I in 499–494 BC. The Persian Empire was still relatively young and prone to revolts amongst its subject peoples.Darius, moreover, was a usurper and had spent considerable time extinguishing revolts against his rule.

The Ionian revolt threatened the integrity of his empire, and Darius thus vowed to punish those involved, especially the Athenians, "since he was sure that [the Ionians] would not go unpunished for their rebellion".Darius also saw the opportunity to expand his empire into the fractious world of Ancient Greece.A preliminary expedition under Mardonius in 492 BC, secured the lands approaching Greece, re-conquered Thrace and forced

Macedon to become a client kingdom of Persia's.

- The Spartans throw Persian envoys into a well

Darius sent emissaries to all the Greek city-states in 491 BC asking for a gift of "earth and water" as tokens of their submission to him.Having had a demonstration of his power the previous year, the majority of Greek cities duly obliged. In Athens, however, the ambassadors were put on trial and then executed by throwing them in a pit; in Sparta, they were simply thrown down a well. This meant that Sparta was also effectively at war with Persia. However, in order to appease the Achaemenid king somewhat, two Spartans were voluntarily sent to Susa for execution, in atonement for the death of the Persian heralds.

Darius thus put together an amphibious task force under Datis and Artaphernes in 490 BC, which attacked Naxos, before receiving the submission of the other Cycladic Islands. The task force then moved on Eretria, which it besieged and destroyed. Finally, it moved to attack Athens, landing at the bay of Marathon, where it was met by a heavily outnumbered Athenian army. At the ensuing Battle of Marathon, the Athenians won a remarkable victory, which resulted in the withdrawal of the Persian army to Asia.

The site of the battle today. Mount Kallidromon on the left, and the wide coastal plain formed by accretion of fluvial deposits over the centuries; the road to the right approximates the 480 BC shoreline.

Darius, therefore, began raising a huge new army with which he meant to completely subjugate Greece; however, in 486 BC, his Egyptian subjects revolted, indefinitely postponing any Greek expedition. Darius then died whilst preparing to march on Egypt, and the throne of Persia passed to his son Xerxes I. Xerxes crushed the Egyptian revolt and very quickly restarted the preparations for the invasion of Greece. Since this was to be a full-scale invasion, it required long-term planning, stockpiling, and conscription.

- Xerxes decided that the Hellespont would be bridged to allow his army to cross to Europe, and that a canal should be dug across the isthmus of Mount Athos (rounding which headland, a Persian fleet had been destroyed in 492 BC). These were both feats of exceptional ambition, which would have been beyond any other contemporary state. By early 480 BC, the preparations were complete, and the army which Xerxes had mustered at Sardis marched towards Europe, crossing the Hellespont on two pontoon bridges. According to Herodotus, Xerxes' army was so large that, upon arriving at the banks of the Echeidorus River, his soldiers proceeded to drink it dry. In the face of such imposing numbers, many Greek cities capitulated to the Persian demand for a tribute of earth and water.

The Athenians had also been preparing for war with the Persians since the mid-480s BC, and in 482 BC the decision was taken, under the guidance of the Athenian politician Themistocles, to build a massive fleet of triremes that would be essential for the Greeks to fight the Persians. However, the Athenians lacked the manpower to fight on both land and sea; therefore, combating the Persians would require an alliance of Greek city-states. In 481 BC, Xerxes sent ambassadors around Greece requesting "earth and water" but very deliberately omitting Athens and Sparta. Support thus began to coalesce around these two leading states. A congress of city-states met at Corinth in late autumn of 481 BC, and a confederate alliance of Greek city-states was formed. It had the power to send envoys to request assistance and dispatch troops from the member states to defensive points, after joint consultation. This was remarkable for the disjointed and chaotic Greek world, especially since many of the city-states in attendance were still technically at war with each other.

The "congress" met again in the spring of 480 BC. A Thessalian delegation suggested that the Greeks could muster in the narrow Vale of Tempe, on the borders of Thessaly, and thereby block Xerxes' advance. A force of 10,000 hoplites was dispatched to the Vale of Tempe, through which they believed the Persian army would have to pass. However, once there, being warned by Alexander I of Macedon that the vale could be bypassed through Sarantoporo Pass and that Xerxes' army was overwhelming, the Greeks retreated. Shortly afterwards, they received the news that Xerxes had crossed the Hellespont.

Themistocles, therefore, suggested a second strategy to the Greeks: the route to southern Greece (Boeotia, Attica, and the Peloponnesus) would require Xerxes' army to travel through the very narrow pass of Thermopylae, which could easily be blocked by the Greek hoplites, despite the overwhelming numbers of Persians. Furthermore, to prevent the Persians from bypassing Thermopylae by sea, the Athenian and allied navies could block the straits of Artemisium. Congress adopted this dual-pronged strategy.However, the Peloponnesian cities made fall-back plans to defend the Isthmus of Corinth, should it come to that, whilst the women and children of Athens would evacuate en masse to the Peloponnesian city of Troezen.

- Prelude

Map showing Greek and Persian advances to Thermopylae and Artemisium

The Persian army seems to have made slow progress through Thrace and Macedon. News of the imminent Persian approach eventually reached Greece in August thanks to a Greek spy. At this time of year the Spartans, de facto military leaders of the alliance, were celebrating the festival of Carneia. During the Carneia, military activity was forbidden by Spartan law; the Spartans had arrived too late at the Battle of Marathon because of this requirement.

- It was also the time of the Olympic Games, and therefore the Olympic truce, and thus it would have been doubly sacrilegious for the whole Spartan army to march to war.On this occasion, the ephors decided the urgency was sufficiently great to justify an advance expedition to block the pass, under one of its kings, Leonidas I. Leonidas took with him the 300 men of the royal bodyguard, the Hippeis. This expedition was to try to gather as many other Greek soldiers along the way as possible and to await the arrival of the main Spartan army.

The legend of Thermopylae, as told by Herodotus, has it that the Spartans had consulted the Oracle at Delphi earlier in the year. The Oracle is said to have made the following prophecy:

"O ye men who dwell in the streets of broad Lacedaemon!
Either your glorious town shall be sacked by the children of Perseus,
Or, in exchange, must all through the whole Laconian country".

- Mourn for the loss of a king, descendant of great Heracles

Herodotus tells us that Leonidas, in line with the prophecy, was convinced he was going to certain death since his forces were not adequate for a victory, and so he selected only Spartans with living sons.

The Spartan force was reinforced en route to Thermopylae by contingents from various cities and numbered more than 7,000 by the time it arrived at the pass.

Leonidas chose to camp at, and defend, the "middle gate", the narrowest part of the pass of Thermopylae, where the Phocians had built a defensive wall some time before. News also reached Leonidas, from the nearby city of Trachis, that there was a mountain track that could be used to outflank the pass of Thermopylae. Leonidas stationed 1,000 Phocians on the heights to prevent such a manoeuvre.

- Leonidas and his companions devoting themselves to death.

Finally, in mid-August, the Persian army was sighted across the Malian Gulf approaching Thermopylae. With the Persian army's arrival at Thermopylae the Greeks held a council of war. Some Peloponnesians suggested withdrawal to the Isthmus of Corinth and blocking the passage to Peloponnesus. The Phocians and Locrians, whose states were located nearby, became indignant and advised defending Thermopylae and sending for more help. Leonidas calmed the panic and agreed to defend Thermopylae. According to Plutarch, when one of the soldiers complained that, "Because of the arrows of the barbarians it is impossible to see the sun", Leonidas replied, "Won't it be nice, then, if we shall have shade in which to fight them?" Herodotus reports a similar comment, but attributes it to Dienekes.

Xerxes sent a Persian emissary to negotiate with Leonidas. The Greeks were offered their freedom, the title "Friends of the Persian People", and the opportunity to re-settle on land better than that they possessed.When Leonidas refused these terms, the ambassador carried a written message by Xerxes, asking him to "Hand over your arms". Leonidas' famous response to the Persians was "Molȍn labé" literally, "having come, take [them]", but usually translated as "come and take them").With the Persian emissary returning empty-handed, battle became inevitable. Xerxes delayed for four days, waiting for the Greeks to disperse, before sending troops to attack them.

- Persian army

For a full discussion of the size of the Persian invasion force, see Second Persian invasion of Greece § Size of the Persian forces.Soldiers of the Achaemenid army of Xerxes I at the time of the Battle of Thermopylae. Tomb of Xerxes I, circa 480 BC, Naqsh-e Rustam.

The number of troops which Xerxes mustered for the second invasion of Greece has been the subject of endless dispute, most notably between ancient sources, which report very large numbers, and modern scholars, who surmise much smaller figures. Herodotus claimed that there were, in total, 2.6 million military personnel, accompanied by an equivalent number of support personnel.The poet Simonides, who was a contemporary, talks of four million; Ctesias gave 800,000 as the total number of the army that was assembled by Xerxes.

Modern scholars tend to reject the figures given by Herodotus and other ancient sources as unrealistic, resulting from miscalculations or exaggerations on the part of the victors. Modern scholarly estimates are generally in the range 120,000–300,000. These estimates usually come from studying the logistical capabilities of the Persians in that era, the sustainability of their respective bases of operations, and the overall manpower constraints affecting them. Whatever the real numbers were, however, it is clear that Xerxes was anxious to ensure a successful expedition by mustering an overwhelming numerical superiority by land and by sea.The number of Persian troops present at Thermopylae is therefore as uncertain as the number for the total invasion force. For instance, it is unclear whether the whole Persian army marched as far as Thermopylae, or whether Xerxes left garrisons in Macedon and Thessaly.

- thank you for buy & read this book

  have a great day of your
  from : Mr Vivek Kumar Pandey

- This All Credit Goes To My Super Hero Daddy. Always Love You dad

Printed by Libri Plureos GmbH in Hamburg, Germany